STAYING
Healthy

By Selina Wood

CELEBRATION PRESS
Pearson Learning Group

The following people from **Pearson Learning Group**
have contributed to the development of this product:

Joan Mazzeo, Dorothea Fox **Design** | **Editorial** Leslie Feierstone Barna, Cindy Kane
Christine Fleming **Marketing** | **Publishing Operations** Jennifer Van Der Heide
Production Laura Benford-Sullivan
Content Area Consultant Amy Keller

The following people from **DK** have
contributed to the development of this product:

Art Director Rachael Foster

Martin Wilson **Managing Art Editor** | **Managing Editor** Marie Greenwood
Polly Appleton **Design** | **Editorial** Selina Wood
Brenda Clynch **Picture Research** | **Production** Gordana Simakovic
Richard Czapnik, Andy Smith **Cover Design** | **DTP** David McDonald
Consultant: Dr. Cornelia Franz M.D.

Dorling Kindersley would like to thank: Anton Deans-Tahir, Jordan Du Maurier, Natasha Tiwari for their help and patience;
Adam Allen, Hannah Burke, Anthony Deans-Tahir, Omar Deans-Tahir, Victoria Deans-Tahir, Beres Dowe, Lisa Du Maurier,
Nabeela Malik, Josh Miller, Emma Newborough, Aneesha Tiwari, and Shammi Tiwari for modelling and assistance;
Gary Ombler for photography; Andy Crawford for additional photography; Alex Pang for illustration;
Rose Horridge in the picture library; Johnny Pau for additional cover design work.

Picture Credits: Science Photo Library: Andrew Syred 24bl.

All other images: DK Dorling Kindersley © 2005. For further information see www.dkimages.com

Special thanks: National Asthma Campaign, Diabetes UK, and Allergies UK;
Langbourne Primary School, Chatham Grammar School for Girls, and King's High School; Dr Buchanan, King's College Hospital, London;
J Sainsbury plc; Crystal Palace National Sports Centre.

ISBN: 0-7652-5252-X

Color reproduction by Colourscan, Singapore
Printed and bound in China by Leo Paper Products Ltd.
1 2 3 4 5 6 7 8 9 10   08 07 06 05 04

1-800-321-3106
www.pearsonlearning.com

Contents

Staying Healthy

Staying healthy is a matter of eating nutritious foods, exercising regularly, and receiving proper medical care. For people with a chronic, or ongoing, disease such as diabetes, allergies, or asthma, staying healthy also involves taking steps to control their illness. A chronic illness is a disease or condition that does not go away and that currently has no cure. Most of these illnesses can be managed with diet, exercise, and medications. This book takes a look at how three children live with diabetes, allergies, and asthma respectively.

Asthma is a condition that affects the respiratory system. The airways, or **bronchial tubes**, narrow and make it difficult to breathe. Asthma attacks can be triggered by **allergens**, strenuous exercise, and very cold or polluted air. About 150 million people around the world have asthma.

Jordan, age eleven, has asthma.

Footnote

Treatments differ from place to place and from person to person. The true stories presented here do not promote specific treatments, but they tell of these children's real experiences.

4

Allergies occur when your body has a negative reaction to something. People can be allergic to many different things. Foods, grass, pollen, dust, and animal **dander** are common allergens. Reactions can range from stuffy noses and itchy eyes to more serious effects, like the inability to breathe. Allergies to nuts, such as cashews, walnuts, and almonds, are among the more serious allergies. Peanuts—a member of the bean family—are responsible for most of the severe allergic reactions to food items.

Diabetes is a disease that causes the body to be unable to process glucose, or sugar, normally. There are a few types of diabetes. Type 1 and Type 2 diabetes are two common forms of this illness. About 177 million people in the world have diabetes, and the numbers are increasing.

Here, you'll read about three young people from the United Kingdom—Anton, who has diabetes, Natasha, who has allergies, and Jordan, who has asthma.

Anton, age nine, has diabetes.

Natasha, age fourteen, has allergies.

Coping With Diabetes

Anton is an active fifth-grader. He loves to play football with his friends and is a great swimmer. Anton also has Type 1 diabetes. This means that his body does not produce insulin, a **hormone** that turns glucose from food into **energy**.

Anton swimming

Types of Diabetes

Type 1

- 5 to 10 percent of all cases of diabetes
- appears mostly in young people
- usually develops quickly
- no insulin produced— treatment requires insulin **injections**

Type 2

- 90 to 95 percent of all cases of diabetes
- appears mostly in overweight adults, forty years and older
- usually develops slowly
- some insulin is produced—treatments include diet and exercise; some people need extra insulin

When Anton was two years old, his mother discovered that he was so thirsty that he had dragged a chair to the sink to drink straight from the tap. Up to this time, Anton seemed to be a healthy little boy. Within a few days, however, he became weak and sleepy. He began to lose weight. He was also using the bathroom often. His worried mother took him to the doctor.

After hearing the **symptoms**, the doctor immediately tested Anton's urine to measure the amount of glucose. Only a blood test could confirm a diabetes **diagnosis**, but the doctor knew that the level of glucose in the urine might point to the problem. The test showed a very high level of glucose in Anton's urine. His case was serious, so the doctor called for an ambulance to take Anton to the hospital. He stayed there for two weeks and was diagnosed with Type 1 diabetes.

All-Important Insulin

In most people, the hormone insulin is produced in an organ called the pancreas. Insulin is important because it controls the amount of glucose that flows in the blood. Anton's body does not produce any insulin because of his Type 1 diabetes, so he must receive insulin shots. Anton's mom gives him the shot before he eats his breakfast and a second one before he eats dinner.

Anton has to follow a regular schedule for his meals and injections. The two work together to keep Anton feeling well. For Anton, injections are as regular as brushing his teeth. After eating, the glucose from his food rushes into his bloodstream. The insulin keeps his blood glucose level from rising too high. On the other hand, if he doesn't have a meal after his injection, his blood glucose level can fall very low. Maintaining a balance between his diet and medication is an important part of Anton's day.

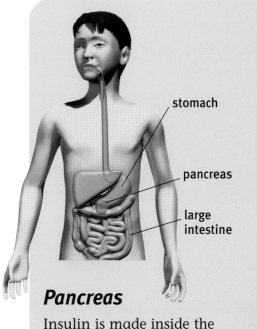

stomach

pancreas

large intestine

Pancreas

Insulin is made inside the pancreas, an organ found behind the stomach.

Anton's diabetes can be treated successfully with injections of insulin.

Managing Diabetes

When Anton wakes up in the morning, he begins his day with a blood glucose level test, so that he knows how much insulin he needs to inject. His mom uses a device with a needle in it to prick his finger. Then a small drop of Anton's blood is placed on a chemically treated strip of paper. A special machine "reads" the strip and tells how much glucose is present in Anton's blood. Regular glucose testing is important because both low and high glucose levels could cause problems. Symptoms of low glucose levels include sweating, nervousness, hunger, and dizziness. Symptoms of high glucose levels include confusion and slurred speech.

Anton's glucose tests help him to monitor his condition.

Anton's School Day

Anton's school day is very much like that of the other children. His favorite subject is design and technology, and he enjoys spending time with his friends. However, Anton must also be aware of his body's signals. He needs to be sure that his glucose level remains in a healthy range throughout the day.

Since Anton takes his insulin shots regularly, his glucose level generally does not get too high, but he also must be careful not to let his level get too low. One way he does this is by having frequent snacks. During his morning recess, Anton usually eats some potato chips. If he forgets, his low glucose level may make him feel dizzy and he may start to shake. If this happens, he must eat right away. He also carries glucose tablets with him at all times. Taking one gives him an immediate boost of sugar to help him feel better fast.

Anton enjoys climbing with his friends during school recess.

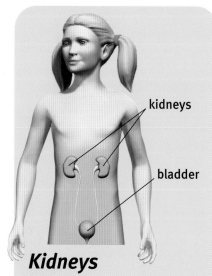

Kidneys

Why do people with untreated diabetes feel so thirsty and have to go to the bathroom frequently? These symptoms occur when there is too much sugar in the blood. The kidneys are trying to filter out the sugar to keep the blood healthy. When the level of glucose rises in the blood, the kidneys can't hold the extra glucose, and it ends up in the urine. Because glucose must dissolve in water in order to exit the body, the kidneys use a large amount of water to get rid of it. Thirst is the body's way of saying it needs this water, so a person with a high glucose level in the blood feels thirsty.

Anton also makes sure to eat a nutritious meal at lunch, usually some starchy foods, such as bread, potatoes, or pasta, along with plenty of vegetables and some meat for protein. Together, these choices provide needed energy to help Anton feel well throughout his school day.

Anton can eat some sugar. However, he must be very careful to make sure it is only a small amount. He doesn't really have much trouble controlling this part of his disease. Anton developed good eating habits early because he had been diagnosed as a diabetic when he was very young. He knows some kids his age who were diagnosed with diabetes later in life. Controlling their diet and trying not to eat sugary foods are real struggles for them. Luckily for Anton, most of his friends have known him for a long time and are aware of his condition. They don't offer him things they know he can't eat.

Glucose comes from the digestion of starchy and sugary foods, such as bread, rice, potatoes, yams, and sweets, such as candy.

Living With Diabetes

One of Anton's favorite activities is swim class. Anton likes many sports, but he is particularly good at swimming. His classmates bring a snack to eat after the lesson because the exercise makes them hungry. For Anton, it is important to eat snacks both before and after the lesson. He usually eats a chocolate bar before strenuous exercise to prevent his blood glucose level from falling too low.

Once every couple of months, Anton must go to the diabetes clinic, a special center at his local hospital, after school. The doctors check his weight, his glucose level, his kidneys, and also his eyesight. The buildup of glucose that occurs in diabetics can have a bad effect on the kidneys and can damage the eyes and even lead to blindness. Anton's doctors help him make adjustments to his routine as his body grows and changes.

Regular exercise is a healthy habit for people with diabetes.

Anton doesn't mind going to the clinic because he meets other people with diabetes there. Talking with people who have the same condition gives Anton support and helps him cope with his illness.

Anton has a full schedule, and like many kids his age, he comes home tired at the end of the day. Anton's mom checks his glucose level again and makes sure he has a snack before he begins his homework. Then his mom prepares a healthy dinner for the family. Before Anton eats, he gets his second insulin injection.

He ends his day with another glucose test and a final bedtime snack. Anton usually sleeps well. Sometimes, though, he wakes up in the middle of the night feeling shaky. Then he has to eat something to raise his glucose level.

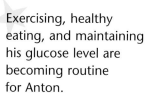

Exercising, healthy eating, and maintaining his glucose level are becoming routine for Anton.

To keep up his active life, Anton has to remember to balance his diet, exercise, maintain his insulin needs, and listen to the signals he receives from his body. Once, while at a friend's birthday party, his mother was busy and Anton was enjoying himself so much that he missed his insulin shot—he had to take it as soon as he remembered. Another time, his mother was held up in traffic and wasn't around to give Anton his evening injection. His friend's mother had to give it to him instead, with Anton's mother giving her instructions over the phone.

Currently, there isn't a cure for diabetes, but that doesn't stop Anton from being positive about the future. He knows that research is ongoing, and a cure could be discovered at any time. Anton dreams of sky diving someday. He knows that having diabetes will not prevent him from achieving his goals.

A diabetic does not have to have special foods. A healthy, well-balanced diet is good for Anton and his family.

Living With a Nut Allergy

Fourteen-year-old Natasha is a typical teenage girl. She loves shopping, reading, and going to see movies with her friends. Natasha is also allergic to many different things, including house dust, pollen, and certain pets. She gets hay fever (an allergy to pollen) in the summer. She has also suffered from a skin rash called eczema since she was two years old. Natasha's most serious allergy is to nuts. She reacts severely whenever she comes into contact with them. Yet, Natasha has learned how to manage her allergies from day-to-day, and she enjoys a very active life.

What Causes Allergies?

No one is sure why some people develop allergies and others do not. Below is a list of theories that some scientists believe may be factors as to why allergies occur.

- Allergies may be inherited, or run in families.
- Allergies may be caused by a virus.
- Environmental changes may lead to more allergies.
- Some scientists feel that we are more sensitive to allergens because we live in cleaner, more insulated environments and are exposed to many types of antibiotics during our life.

Natasha's favorite breakfast is a bowl of fresh fruit.

A First Diagnosis

Natasha was only five years old when she had her first major reaction to nuts. She had a new breakfast cereal, which contained nuts, and went off to school. After an hour or so, she began to feel sick. Her face became swollen, her lips were tingling, and it was difficult for her to breathe because her throat was swelling up. Natasha was rushed to the hospital and lost consciousness soon after arriving there. A team of doctors and nurses started to revive her. They were about to give her a shot of **adrenaline** when she came around. Natasha fully recovered. She was very lucky!

During a skin test, the doctor scratches a tiny drop of allergen onto the skin with a special device.

Doctors told Natasha and her mother that she had experienced a severe, life-threatening allergic reaction. The doctors traced her allergy to the nuts in her cereal. They told Natasha to avoid eating nuts in the future. That meant she had to check the ingredients of everything she ate, which is often a difficult job. The doctors made some additional tests on her skin to see what other allergens she might be sensitive to. The results showed that she was allergic to many things.

Allergy to nuts is increasingly common.

Some Symptoms of Allergic Reaction

- swollen face, lips, and tongue
- difficulty breathing
- itchy, red rash
- light-headedness, sometimes unconsciousness

Mast Cell

Mast cells are located in the skin, nose, and other areas of the body. The first time the body's mast cells are exposed to an allergen, they build up **antibodies**.

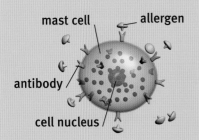

mast cell   allergen

antibody

cell nucleus

1. Antibodies produced during the cell's first exposure to allergens attach to the surface of the cell.

2. Allergens come in contact with antibodies during later exposure.

histamine

3. The contact of allergens with antibodies causes the cell to release histamine, producing an allergic reaction.

Controlling the Allergens

Natasha's reactions to some allergens, such as nuts, can be life-threatening. As a result, she must carry medicines with her in case of an emergency. Natasha's doctors have trained her in how to recognize the symptoms of an attack and how to use the medicines in her pack to handle emergency situations.

If Natasha feels an allergic reaction coming on, the first thing she does is take an antihistamine tablet, which blocks her body's allergic response. If she has difficulty breathing, she uses an **inhaler** to help her breathe more easily. If the attack is severe and won't stop, she uses an Epi-Pen™—an auto-injector for life-threatening allergic reactions—to inject herself with epinephrine, or adrenaline. Adrenaline increases the flow of blood through the body and flushes the allergens from her system.

Her pack contains various creams that can help if she develops a skin rash. Natasha also wears a bracelet to let people know about her allergies in case she passes out. This can happen when the histamines released cause a sudden drop in blood pressure.

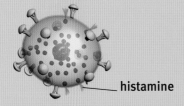

Natasha wears a medical-alert bracelet.

Natasha's School Day

On a typical morning, Natasha has a healthy breakfast and gets ready for school. Some mornings she feels the effects of her allergies, especially as spring comes and the amount of pollen in the air increases. If she notices her body giving her signals, such as itchy eyes, congestion, or headache, she takes allergy medicine. With her symptoms improved, Natasha will have an easier time concentrating on her schoolwork. The last thing she does before leaving the house is check her emergency medical pack, which she carries everywhere she goes.

Natasha at the age of five

antihistamine tablets

Epi-Pen™

Natasha's emergency pack includes an Epi-Pen™, an inhaler, antihistamine tablets, and three types of cream to treat skin rashes.

inhaler

creams

Allergy	Symptoms	Allergen
hay fever	runny nose, itchy eyes	pollen
eczema	itchy, reddened skin	dust mites, stress, pets, chemicals, detergents
asthma	wheezing, difficulty breathing	dust mites, pollen, mold, pet dander, tobacco smoke, certain medicines, exercise, stress, cold air
food allergies	swelling of the lips, hives, digestive tract symptoms, dizziness, sometimes unconsciousness	certain foods
bee/wasp sting	red rash, asthma, dizziness, sometimes unconsciousness	bee or wasp sting

With her medicines checked, Natasha is off to school. Her schedule is much like that of her fellow classmates. She takes a variety of classes and studies hard, especially when it is time for exams. For lunch, Natasha eats with her friends in the school lunchroom. She does check with the lunchroom staff to make sure that no nuts are in the meal that she wants to eat. She usually has pizza or pasta. Three other students at her school have nut allergies, so the school is well prepared.

Some people are allergic to grass pollen, but Natasha's body doesn't react to grass. However, the pollen of some trees may cause hay fever.

After school, Natasha loves to go shopping with her mother and younger sister. Sometimes, they stop for a snack. When Natasha eats out, she always asks the server what ingredients are in the food before she orders from the menu and keeps the emergency kit handy, just in case.

Food is not the only thing that Natasha needs to be concerned about on her shopping trip. She must also carefully read the labels on other items, such as shampoo and beauty products. These items sometimes contain nuts or oils from nuts. If Natasha decides to wear makeup in the future, she will also need to check those labels. Several kinds of lipstick use oil from nuts as an ingredient. Fortunately, now many companies are placing warnings on their labels to notify consumers that nut ingredients are used in the product.

Natasha looks at the ingredients of things she buys— including shampoo!

On the weekends, Natasha spends time with her friends. Sometimes, they get together and talk about their favorite bands or the latest movies. Natasha always makes sure to put her medicines into her handbag before going out.

Wherever she goes with her friends, Natasha must be aware of the food being served. If nuts are present, she must be very careful. Natasha's nut allergy is so severe that she may have a reaction just from having physical contact with people who have eaten nuts. At a party a few years ago, she hugged and kissed her relatives who had been eating peanuts, and she had a bad reaction. Now she is very careful all the time.

When Natasha gets ready to go out, she puts her medical kit into her bag.

Natasha enjoys hiking trips with her friends.

Natasha enjoys hiking and camping. There is one hiking trip she still laughs about! She and her hiking group had been walking for miles, and they were tired. They stopped for lunch under a tree. Halfway through lunch, someone noticed that the tree they were resting under was a horse chestnut, a type of nut tree. The whole group got up and ran away! Natasha was okay, though. She didn't have an allergic reaction that time.

Many food allergies, particularly nut allergies, are lifelong. Natasha has learned to live with her condition and to avoid eating nuts. Her allergies don't affect her most of the time, and she has learned to read the signals her body gives her, which warn her about a potential problem. By being aware of her surroundings, paying attention to the food she eats and the products she uses, and staying prepared in case of an emergency, Natasha successfully manages her allergies and enjoys her life.

Symptoms of Asthma

- wheezing
- shortness of breath
- difficulty inhaling and exhaling
- coughing
- sweating

Kicking Asthma

Jordan, an eleven-year-old seventh grader, has a passion for martial arts. He takes part in martial arts classes and enjoys kickboxing. He has even won a large collection of trophies in martial arts competitions and for running. However, Jordan is different from some other competitors. He lives with a condition called asthma.

When a person has asthma, the air passages inside the lungs become irritated and swollen. When the passages swell, the airways become narrower, making it hard to breathe. Some of the symptoms during an asthma attack include coughing, shortness of breath, a tight feeling in the chest, and a whistling sound during breathing called wheezing. Jordan's asthma requires him to take special steps each day to keep him healthy and allow him to breathe comfortably.

Jordan has won more than thirty trophies for martial arts and running.

Managing Asthma

Jordan experienced wheezing when he was just a baby. However, his symptoms gradually settled down. A few years later, when he was seven, he ran out of breath while running. He had always been very energetic. Suddenly, he couldn't run because he felt his chest tighten up and he couldn't breathe. He couldn't perform in sports as well as he used to, so he felt very frustrated. He would also develop more severe breathing problems each time he caught a cold, because the excess mucus from the cold triggered his asthma.

After an asthma attack at school, Jordan was sent to the hospital. The doctor had him use a nebulizer, a machine that allows a liquid medicine to be inhaled as a mist. The medicine relaxes and widens the airways and relieves asthma symptoms.

The doctor also gave him a medicine to reduce the swelling of his airways. This was the first step in managing Jordan's asthma.

What Is Asthma?

Asthma is a long-term chronic condition that affects the lungs.
- The airways are narrowed.
- The airways are inflamed.
- The inflamed airways produce too much mucus, a protective liquid that coats the inner lining of the airways.
- The airways are overly sensitive to many different triggers.

Normal Airway

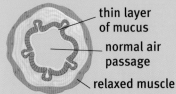

- thin layer of mucus
- normal air passage
- relaxed muscle

Constricted Airway

- excess mucus
- narrowed air passage
- contracted muscle

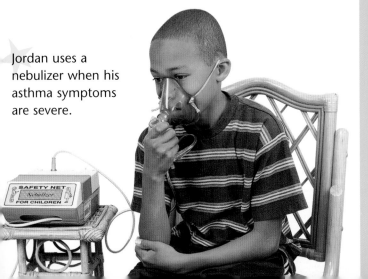

Jordan uses a nebulizer when his asthma symptoms are severe.

Jordan's School Day

Jordan begins his day with a puff of medication from his inhaler. This medication helps keep his airways relaxed and open and makes it less likely that he will have an asthma attack during the day. Unfortunately, it doesn't guarantee that he will not experience problems from his asthma, especially when the weather is cold.

Cold air is one of the things that can trigger some people's symptoms of asthma. Jordan must be especially careful during the coldest times of the year. Cold weather requires him to use a different inhaler and to use it more often. This inhaler has a reliever drug which relaxes the muscles around his airways and helps him breathe properly. Jordan makes sure to have his relief inhaler with him all the time.

What Causes Asthma?

Asthma tends to run in families, but what triggers it and how intense the attacks are varies from person to person. Asthma can be a reaction to air pollution, cigarette smoke, perfume, or the remains of dust mites that live in mattresses and carpets in the home. It may also be triggered by the excess mucus production associated with a cold or viral infection.

This dust mite has been magnified many times, because a dust mite cannot be seen with the naked eye.

By using a relief inhaler, Jordan can breathe more easily.

Jordan's school day is very much like that of other children. He takes many different classes, but he really loves science. His asthma does not require him to follow a special diet, so he is able to eat whatever he likes during his lunch break. Jordan knows what it feels like when he begins to have an asthma attack, so by listening to signals from his body, he is able to prevent a serious attack from occurring. Jordan really enjoys spending time with his friends and playing sports.

Jordan conducts science experiments at school.

For a while after he was diagnosed, Jordan sat on the sidelines while his friends played soccer. He was worried that he would not be able to breathe. He also felt a little shy about using his inhaler in front of his friends. Then one day he went to see a former world champion kickboxer at his local sports center.

Jordan is a champion kickboxer.

The kickboxer was an incredible speaker, and his attitude toward sports inspired Jordan. After hearing the kickboxer speak, Jordan decided to find out how he could be active and try the sports that interested him, while managing his asthma. Jordan talked with his doctor and made a plan for dealing with his symptoms while exercising. Then he decided to take up martial arts as a hobby. Since then, he has also begun participating in kickboxing and even cross-country running.

Jordan practices his martial arts.

Communicating With the Doctor

It is important for asthma patients to communicate, or talk, with their doctors. Patients need to discuss how to deal with their specific symptoms. Here are some ways patients effectively work with their doctors.

- Ask questions and express their concerns about their condition.
- Tell the doctor about their goals and ask for advice on the healthiest, safest ways to achieve them.
- Keep notes of any symptoms or problems and share that information with the doctor.

After school, Jordan goes to martial arts practice. He also frequently competes in tournaments. During a tournament, Jordan faces several opponents. The matches are held in a large gymnasium with an audience cheering him on. Jordan makes sure that he follows his special routines to keep himself healthy during the match.

27

Before he competes, Jordan blows air into a machine called a peak flow meter. This device measures the rate of air that comes out of his lungs. Jordan can use this information to determine whether his lungs are functioning well. Normally, Jordan's air flow reading is well above average because he is so fit from all of his sports training. However, before a competition, he often finds his reading is only average because he is nervous.

About fifteen minutes before his first competition, Jordan usually takes a puff of his relief inhaler. This prevents him from wheezing and helps keep his chest from feeling tight. Because the competitions are long and involve many matches, he sometimes feels asthma symptoms in the middle of a tournament. If this occurs, Jordan takes a few puffs from his inhaler, and within a few minutes, he breathes normally again.

A peak flow meter can be used to measure Jordan's breathing capacity.

Jordan runs cross-country.

Jordan won't let his asthma get in the way of his passion for sports. In fact, the more exercise he does, the less he relies on his inhalers. He follows his doctors' instructions, and has learned to listen to the signals he receives from his body. Jordan knows that asthma is a condition that requires him to be alert to these signals, and he is prepared to deal with them. He no longer feels self-conscious of his need to take the medications that keep him breathing well.

His love of sports has given him the courage to learn to manage his asthma. He has won sports scholarships, and, amazingly, has run more than 3 miles in 18 minutes. Now his ambition is to be in the movies—preferably martial arts movies. Jordan really has given asthma a kung fu chop!

Jordan plans to win many more trophies in the future.

29

Conclusion

Living with a chronic condition such as diabetes, allergies, or asthma does not have to mean giving up fun and exciting opportunities. Anton, Natasha, and Jordan each face challenges with their health. They also each prove that with education, good health care, and loving, supportive families, they can develop the tools necessary to manage their conditions successfully.

Each of these children shows us how important it is to keep a positive attitude and to stay strong. Even when things are difficult or uncomfortable, they have found ways to meet the challenges they face. They are determined to manage their illnesses and to stay healthy.

Jordan, Anton, and Natasha have great plans for the future.

Glossary

adrenaline   a hormone produced by the body at times of stress or excitement that makes the heart pump blood through the body faster; it may be injected into the body to revive someone who is unconscious

allergens   substances that produce an allergic reaction

antibodies   special proteins in the body made by white blood cells that fight germs and other foreign substances

bronchial tubes   tubes that branch off from a larger airway called the trachea and go deep into each lung

dander   small scales of hair, feathers, or skin

diagnosis   a decision about a patient's disease that is formed after checking symptoms and taking tests

energy   the body's fuel needed for action

hormone   a substance produced by the body to have an effect on other parts of the body (such as to start growth or to control glucose level)

inhaler   an instrument used for breathing in medicine

injections   medicines forced into the body with syringes

symptoms   bodily reactions that indicate a disease

Index